Being like water

By

Charlie Fox

www.charliefox.biz

ISBN 978-0-9564997-2-1

Published by Charlie Fox

Visit my website at www.charliefox.biz

First Printing: September 2009

"No one should fool himself. If anyone among you thinks he is wise by this world's standards, he should become a fool, in order to be really wise."

(1 Corinthians 3: The holy Bible)

"...Be water my friend."

(Bruce Lee)

Contents: pg

Foreword

'Being like water' is essentially six years worth of thoughts, dreams, considerations, realisations and points of discussion which eventually developed and cohesed into something more holistic and directed.

The overriding theme of this book is that following the gospel of Christ is the most effective way of adapting to the world and events in your life. It is an attempt to explain WHY this works and why it changes people's lives for the better every day. Also to place the belief system into a wider contemporary spiritual context.

I have divided this document into chapters, but there may be repetition and intersection from one chapter into another and so I leave it up to you reader, in some ways, to join the dots.

It jumps about slightly and some subjects come in from left field, especially in 'The rest' section. I have chosen to leave these in for character and due to the spirit in which the book was written.

To the Father,

and my son.

For all the people in my life, that is, all of you.

And for Helen.

Actual Christianity

True Christianity is personal Christianity. You walking with Christ. It is not organised religion.

Christianity's power is not immediate and self - gratifying, it is progressive and gives personal freedom. Immediate, unearned power which is self gratifying has a price and leaves you in bondage to desires of your own ego.

Many people say they cannot follow Christ because they cannot see him.

Let us pretend for a moment that following Christ means constantly satisfying all your physical desires with whomever you wish and all morality being a matter of personal choice.

Then let us say that materialism is a belief system which promotes monogamy and forgiveness of your enemies. If this were true how many then would follow Christ? Following Christ is the hardest road and that is why people do not follow him, it is not because they cannot see him.

True Christianity's focus is on developing character and spirit through adaptation, not sating the desires of your ego. It prepares you for the next world, and does not allow you to waste yourself in this one.

As a man Jesus is dead and gone. As God you can FEEL him in your spirit, if you try.

Only God is God, the bible is a book ABOUT God.

Real Christianity is not a mind controlling trap, though some people may twist and use it as such, even some churches. This, sadly, in many people's minds, destroys the validity of Christ's message.

Scripture takes second place to actual action in that following Christ is about leading through service to others, not leading through trying to control how they think and feel.

God uses those who have faith. If you have faith, it makes real your relationship with God.

Be aware that many people's experience of what Christianity is has been coloured and soured by the church. The antics of the church establishment have turned many people from Christ. Christianity is not the church. Christianity is nothing more than a personal relationship with God manifested through your actions, choices, prayers and through relationships with other people. It is both internal and external in nature, as God is both internal and external in nature. This means that answers to prayer can come either externally or internally.

People will recognise God when they are ready.

No amount of aggressive poking, prodding or 'bible bashing' will persuade them otherwise and may indeed drive them away. You could be doing a definite disservice.

Give them an option, demonstrate the benefits through your own actions and let them CHOOSE. You cannot convict someone of their own sins, they must do that themselves.

Choosing to walk with God must be a FULL PERSONAL choice.

The great challenge of Christianity is knowing what to do under your own power and what to leave to God. Therefore you must have faith in yourself as well as faith in God.

The acid test of any doctrine is how it performs outside of its own institution.

The true power of God can only be seen by those who can set their own aside. Maybe you can do right by others and not believe in God but can you do right by yourself and not believe in God? (If you cannot do right by yourself first how can you do right by others? God holds the perfect path to your life).

Jesus dying for past sins is symbolic; dying to prove further sin worthless is actual Christianity.

It is about sacrifice of one's ego.

Sin is walking your own path, not Gods.

Since God knows your perfect path through life and that of others, if you walk your own you cannot avoid hurting yourself and others along the way. Attempting to do Gods will for your life will limit the damage you do to yourself and others.

Taking away Christian ministry and mission from many developed and undeveloped countries would be disastrous to the social services of those countries. The extent of support these services give cannot be underestimated.

Christians cry and get depressed like everyone else. It doesn't mean their faith doesn't work, solving personal issues and problems in one's life if usually progressive but Christianity gives much ENDURANCE. Spiritual people recognise more than others the benefits and function of freely expressing negative emotions.

Christianity is about suspending your judgement of others, not accelerating it.

Envision Jesus as a perfected version of you and not as a remote historical figure. If not you, someone from your community living a similar life to you, whether you are male or female. His body was not his spirit. He is the inspiration to our own perfection.

If you don't believe that Jesus is the son of God, take the risk of living as he did for a time. By the time you've seen the positive change in yourself and felt peace enter your life you may very well experience that as truth.

When speaking of Christ, never speak in terms of religion. Never use religious figures of speech which will scare, exclude and confound the truth seeking soul. Speak with simplicity, tolerance and directness, as he did.

Christ's message was one of love, but with responsibility. Real love is responsible.

Worship is never abusive to others, or to God. If you live your life to God's plan and influenced by the gospel of Jesus, that is an act of worship which can never then be abusive to others or to God.

Following Christ reveals the world to you and you to the world naked of your illusions of personal power.

God uses situations that WE get ourselves into to teach us lessons we need.

Christianity is the art of making the most unselfish and often most difficult choices in any given situation.

Christianity is a constant fearless taking of self inventory, analysis and making change. There is no standing still as the world does not stand still.

To be an effective Christian, emotionally and mindfully you must be constantly adaptive. 'Be like water'.

Christianity is a mirror. It reflects violence and injustice and iniquity onto normal-minded perpetrators through a non- reaction and a righteous state of guiltlessness from the victim. This is one of the greatest lessons of the crucifixion.

Such a display of self sacrifice of power and lack of retaliation from the most sinless, perfect yet powerful being in the universe automatically convicts the guilty in their own minds through comparison, (CONVICTION of self through displaying positive example and using a policy of non condemnation - allowing evil to take its course to its useless and decrepit end).

Look at the wisdom inherent in a system. People stop looking at Christianity because of the ' male and female' problem, that god is seen as male, that Jesus was male and because of the roles of males in the church. This then is taken by paganism as a way to convert through empowerment of the female gender. This is all a side issue, Jesus life and teachings apply to all of us, whether male or female, and gender issues and empowerment is a distraction from this. Look at the life of Jesus first, and then step back and look at the circumstances in which it took place.

Christ's way involves changing one's life. Leaving behind what is wrong and harmful, not allowing one to continue to do such negative things by offering a new way of seeing things- as eastern religions do.

Christianity deconstructs and then reconstructs you as a new being continuously improving and purging.

Eastern religions allow you to stay the same through offering a new perspective, thus they can allow wrong actions to remain.

Christianity offers a great deal of hard work.

Christianity is the most effective world religion as it causes you to change and adapt constantly. Through alignment of choice to the will of God through prayer.

Contemporary Christianity is based upon a sacred covenant of guilt. Rather it should extol virtue than punish transgression as this is a far more effective manner of teaching than making numb unthinking followers through a literally glorified form of aversion training.

The church is not REPRESENTATIVE of Christ; instead it is a grouping of people who wish to EMULATE Christ surrounded by a HUMAN power structure which like all power structures is open to abuse.

Conversely Christ taught love and adaptation whereas all too often the church in Christ's name has taught fear and control. Therefore the church should not be confused with Christ and the church should not be confused with the fallible people within it.

The church is therefore the faceless organisation of individuals wishing to emulate Christ. Blaming individuals for the crimes of the church is fallacious. The church is the gun not the person pulling the trigger, thus is the danger of organised religion.

It then becomes politicised and a movement of earthly power rather than a manifestation of the kingdom (a spiritual movement).

To avoid this, the church should be representative of individuals who are answerable to their own faiths and personal direct relationship with God only, not a group organised under a formulised power structure of priests, bishops, ministers and various 'religiously anointed middle men'.

Any individual who has been recognised in the group as having leadership qualities should be termed 'advisor/facilitator???' and not placed within an official role. If he naturally occupies that role, it will always be recognised anyway, leadership should be organic and title incidental as a result of the role already played.

Always remember, Christ is about leading through service to others.

Do not let a church bind your spirit. Be a church.

Views on the crucifixion

You must not try and create fear and slavery from a message of freedom and emancipation.

Can you forgive yourself for hurting yourself? Or can only God as your creator?

God wants to be made the recipient of the weight of our sins. Each time we hurt ourselves through our own actions, and the guilt of hurting others, we carry this with us. Forgiveness of ourselves can free us from this. The crucifixion is to make us aware of our own sins. It tells us that God himself understands and will bear the weight for us, if we give it to him by recognising that Christ sacrificed himself on the cross, the perfect being, to expose our imperfectness and by comparison see how imperfect our lives are. Jesus died to make us see this. So we had a measure, to compare our lives with his own. How hard is it for a loving parent to educate his erring children who are harming themselves and the parent? How do you teach them but through consequence, but to let them make their own mistakes? So the Romans were left by God to kill Jesus.

How do you teach a million? A billion?

Often we do not know why we hurt ourselves & others. We are not outside ourselves & so cannot be objective. God is outside & inside us all so he knows & will take the painful weight of our wrong choices if we allow it.

Like in Alcoholics anonymous where they 'give it to God' you simply extend this to include every negative tendency in your life you know needs addressing. Ultimately you owe it to yourself, no one else.

You must recognise these things as being wrong to do, if you persist in doing them, you cannot be helped.

We all know the principle that we must let people make their own mistakes, to learn. God allowed Jesus to be crucified to let the world learn its mistake and by killing ultimate good in the place of ultimate evil, recognise its own iniquity.

We should not see our own perfect paths being crucified for the world's sake.
Perpetual sin against one's self and others ends with the destruction of one's life.

Do not be slavishly controlled by the desires of this world, be dynamically and brilliantly driven to best it.

The crucifixion shows us the consequences of human iniquity. We do not have to go there. It depicts the death of eternal values through the short term destruction of violence & the resurrection of them thru long term creativity- forgiveness.

God is a beneficent god and a loving father, not a childish fear inducing control freak. The crucifixion is a demonstration of how iniquity and sin do not work. The story of Judas Iscariot and his ignominious downfall to his own ego and consequent suicide prove this.

Selling something as perfect as love and truth away for material wealth is a denial of Christ's message and his purpose on earth.

Above all, the crucifixion and resurrection was the ultimate act of love and how it conquers and destroys sin. It was not a threat to make slaves of mankind. It was to demonstrate to us the principles of a successful life.

It is not as if God wants to impose a plan upon us which is wrong and will make us unhappy. When we sin, or go away from his path, we are mostly just hurting ourselves. Many people seem to have to push sin as far as it will go to find happiness.

They never find it because the desires of their own ego lead them around in a vicious downward spiral of dissatisfaction.

Because they cannot see outside themselves and those desires they cannot see the bigger picture. As soon as we begin to sin we yearn to find again the perfect path. Ourselves in relation to the truth.

Although children are innocent and exploratory during the first stages of life there does come a time of their first MORAL decision when they are fully capable of recognizing right and wrong. So past this point a child can still walk its own path.

If you need to be more selfish, god will teach you how to do that also. Some people forget to take care of themselves in life. God is in favour of perfect BALANCE in us.

Repentance is just knowing that we did the wrong thing and admitting it. Proclaiming it out loud, in whatever small way, to God and the world. This makes it actual and complete, rather than just a thought.

Jesus was killed by man because he was perfect.Encountering perfection can produce inspiration and love or frustration, anger and hate.

Grace

Extending Grace to others allows you to detach from material (short term) desires and extend your appreciation of spiritual (long term) values by taking you further into the kingdom of God and away from the ego.

When you have the grace to ask for blessings for someone else this detaches you from the desires of your own ego.

The ego wants immediate power. Domination of personality over circumstance and environment and relationship. The exaltation of the self.

The material world (money, possessions, false power) provide this. It allows man to adapt his environment to his whim but does not develop the adaptation to environment technique necessary for true spiritual character. That is:

Appreciation of values, not things - people (personalities), not power.

Over materialism stunts spiritual growth through convenience and stagnation of comfort - (no struggle) and produces a state of ennui.

Instead of 'bad' and 'good' think - 'not of the kingdom' and 'of the kingdom'. 'Bad' and 'good' are subjective and do not take into account the benefits to character building and appreciation of spiritual (long - term) values that can accrue through adapting and moving past difficult life hurdles.

So not 'good things happen to good people' only 'things happen to people'. How they deal with them is the point.

Materially orientated people are more likely not to be blessed internally as they lack the vision, patience and insight to learn the character lessons from a difficult event in their lives, though such an event can bring sudden awareness and appreciation of spiritual values. If though they attempt to solve the problem through more short- term and immediate measures (alcohol, drugs, sex, spending, addictions) at the expense of these values they will fail.

Often you cannot see the good that has happened to people in their lives. You cannot initially see the fruits of the spirit that come from learning and withstanding tribulation such as more patience, more faith, and more capacity for love in the same way that you can a new house, more money, more leisure time, expensive clothing and luxury goods that confer status in the material world.

When people say that good things only happen to bad people they are generally only referring to those things that are immediately obvious.

Good things only happen to anyone if they learn from them. The good thing is the reaction. Therefore good only flows from bad if you allow it.

'Karma'

There is a difference between cause and effect and karma, that being the belief in reincarnation - very different, in real karma, there is no forgiveness, your sins will be reflected in the form of your next life.

The concept of karma is false as there is no learning from making a mistake you cannot remember from a previous life.

There is no redeeming or putting that mistake right as a result under these conditions.

No-one can tell you what those sins were, though to abuse their power some priests of karmic belief systems may attempt to do so.

Short term/Long term

Short term values are for maintenance of immediate situation only but this is very necessary. To ignore your short term needs is as bad as ignoring your long term ones. However, do not sacrifice your long term character goals as a result.

───────────────────────

Violence is short term and destructive. Forgiveness is long term and creative.

───────────────────────

Evil is not long sighted, it deals only in the short term, does not promote personal change but in changing the environment instead so again no adaptation.

It keeps the world's vision fixed on the short term through the constant promises of the media and advertising industries to make life better through material products and services in partnership with the desires of the ego to give the illusion of control of their lives to many people. But if you take away their possessions they cannot cope because they have no appreciation of SELF, they are always projecting it onto THINGS. This is not of the kingdom of God which is constant learning, adaptation to change and appreciation and fostering of long term character values such as patience, tolerance, forgiveness.

───────────────────────

Short term pleasure seeking is about manipulating chemical reactions from the brain which is decidedly material, adrenalin, and serotonin, endorphins, from drugs, casual sex, extreme sports and risk taking, stealing, anti-authoritarianism in some forms. All short term highs which never balance properly and become addictive. Body, not spirit focused.

―――――――――――――――――――――――

Religions and belief systems that promote influencing of the environment and the law of attraction and reject God, indeed encouraging each of us to be our own God, discount whether what you desire to attract is any good for you at that point in your life, there is a danger that the ego will take over and desire only short term satisfactions like power, sex and money. God gives you things when they will prove to be good for you in your life and you are ready for them. We know the beginning of something but God also knows the end. If you use the law of attraction in conjunction with prayer and through God to manifest things in your life, you will always receive what is optimal for you, just what you need, nothing more and nothing less.

―――――――――――――――――――――――

Beneficial in the long term/spiritual choices break the chains of depression though the tendency when depressed is toward that which reinforces the vicious circle, to try and cope through short term choices such as alcohol/ casual sex/ drugs/ crime etc.

Short term solutions are often evil in nature and are mostly born of avoidance to change and growth. (Short term solutions are material and not spiritual in nature).

+————————————————

Materialism and short term solutions, pro-consumption, society isolates the individual or the mass for control. To beat 'the system', small communities must be maintained.

+————————————————

Things, desires and needs to be fulfilled and abilities will come in their own time and when you are ready for them, do not try and force them nor pretend you are ready for them when you are not, you cannot pre-empt maturity in yourself.

+————————————————

Living for the moment is a good thing; living for the moment at the expense of the future is not.

+————————————————

Long term solutions are generally more spiritual in nature.

+————————————————

Short term solutions are just that - short term, and trying to use them as long term solutions is like viewing the boy with his finger in the dam as a permanent solution to the problem.

Short term solutions can also spawn addictions and addictive behaviour and foster avoidance of change.

Becoming a Christian levels you out so you no longer are pushed from pillar to post, it is a case of the hare and the tortoise, Christians do not risk so much damage to themselves. A sacred path also highlights and draws ever more distinct divisions between what God wants and what you want. Though the mind is less prey to this abstinence of stimulation and temptation the body is not as strong and may take a while to catch up.

Morality

True consistently accurate morality lies only in the Fathers will.

Conscious consideration of the human relative concepts of good and evil requires much effort and results in a kind of double mindedness.

Instead seek the Father's will, the voice of God lying with your spirit which carries with it the perfect plan for your life as well as a perfect moral decision for each situation.

The spiritual mind must not then be torn in discerning good and evil which is a distraction in relativity.

It must (the mind) battle only with the stimulations of the world, and the electro chemical urges of the body to attain discernment of the small still voice of the eternal spirit within.

Given the right circumstances, anyone can become anything, do not judge and make humans with damaging experiences into monsters. The experience that damaged is the monster. The range of human experience is very wide, helping to normalize monstrous experiences helps kill the monster and humanizes the sufferer.

The chakra system is directly linked to the mind and moral choice.

Material choices emphasise the material body and world and so the lower chakras and arrest the natural progressive energy rise through the chakra system of the body which is the energetic manifestation of spiritual attainment and moral choice - spiritual development. This cannot be affected in any other way - forced - without causing illness and imbalance in character, behaviour or body.

Therefore wilful and non-moral purely self serving and ultimately self retarding choices will stunt, labour and possibly distort spiritual growth.

The only way to truly empower oneself is through proper use and development of your morals and virtues. That is the only way to be beautiful, not through some random genetic identity such as race or perceived social class.

Prayer

Pray for values, not things, pray for endurance, strength, patience, temperance, kindness, love. God is spirit minded and he wishes you to conquer the material world with your spirit so he will help you. If you really need material things to help you do this, he will grant these as well. God is very aware of necessities but he is not someone who will grant needless luxuries which will encourage lassitude and laziness and therefore stunt spiritual progress.

Spiritual development is a gradual process, don't expect to get there straight away, each of us have many base tendencies and potential addictive behaviours to work through. The watchwords here are patience and steadiness. Passionate endurance.

Jesus tarried long in the wilderness to find the Father's will.

Do not be impatient with yourself. Each and every sincere effort to discern the Father's will shall be answered and more clearly each time as long as you bend your will to the achievement of it.

The human voice is a powerful tool. Creative. We create situations in our lives with it. It carries with it our intention and the world is responsive to it so we should be careful what we say.

This is one reason why we should talk to god in private. We can say anything to him.

Confession also plays its part. A problem shared is truly a problem halved. Problems left only in the mind can be magnified out of all proportion, they have nowhere to go. Releasing them to others gives them proper context and allows the mind to flow and react externally with the world again.

Be alive and in harmony with the present, not stuck in the past. Only God though can give absolution. Not a man.

Reflectivity/Adaptation

Because we are reflective beings, we can hide from our pain until it is reflected back at us by someone else-hence our desire to be isolated at bad times, it is pure avoidance. The human mind is a mirror, and our eyes provide the window.

As water reflects the world in reverse, try withdrawing from what you desire, trying yielding to power instead of opposing it. This philosophy of an opposite reaction to what your immediate reaction can be is very good spiritual training.

Doing the opposite only applies when dealing with people. Depressing the primal reaction and enforcing that of spiritual choice. In the physical world, cause and effect is positive in nature, you throw a stone and it flies through the air, science governs our physical world. The world can be manipulated and controlled in this way. When dealing with people this process is more or less reversed, you cannot force anyone to willingly do your will, they will want to do the opposite to what you command, as a child does if told they cannot do this over and over again, that it is forbidden.

It is the wrong EMPHASIS and is an attempt to negate their choice and free will. Even God himself does not rob us of our free will, because he loves us, so we should not attempt to rob others of theirs, however much we are concerned for them.

Emphasise good choices for people. Let them choose.

The sick man on the street needs people, not cold philosophy. To expose problems due to the laws of reflectivity we need others. One cannot self diagnose all the time.

To help ourselves we need others due to the law of reflectivity. Need others to reflect and so know ourselves. Lack of others leads to no knowledge of self and so perceived loss of self (madness).

'Can a stone become smooth on its own?'

Characterful association with like and unlike minds causes increased personality capacity for adaptation, compromise and love through understanding. Like the stone made smooth through constant erosion against other stones (of various hardnesses and sizes) in the ocean which reaches its optimal shape to operate within the group without suffering more damage.

A good teacher is a reflector, a mirror, we all learn about ourselves through reflection from others.

Adaptation and alignment through acceptance is healing.

A refusal to adapt and change is evil in nature as such an attitude is an attempt to stay the same and to change the world to your own desires rather than to adapt to events you cannot change and GROW by overcoming them. It betrays an unhealthy love of one's own power and an incapability to live within boundaries.

Water does everything at once. If you do everything at once you do nothing but become a possibility of everything. It is a state of readiness. Readiness to adapt.

We all reflect one another and so we need others to define ourselves.

Marriage is a supreme exercise in adaptation, learning to compromise and move forward with someone else as though two were one. Through getting to know someone else on such an intimate level, you get to know yourself. Marriage also explores the male and female roles and their differences and balances them outside in the relationship with the spouse and also inside yourself.

The way to be happy is to recognise happiness in the present moment not just through hindsight or as a desire for the future. Happiness lies in dealing appropriately with what is thrown at you. If you deal with it well, you can be happy. If you do not, you cannot.

Emphasis

Emphasis is a tool for self improvement and eradication of unhelpful and/or unhealthy traits. Emphasise the good in others and the good in oneself. Emphasise the good in one another; the world is a mirror than reflects back at you what you put out into it. When self image is thus improved so is self worth and consequent validity of character.

When you emphasise the good rather than condemning the bad, as in effective child rearing or in any kind of character nurturing, eventually, the good will crowd out the bad.

Politics and spirituality

Political values change to suit each situation but spiritual values are permanent and unchanging.

Political correctness depends on the desire to be liked. It makes people scared to expose their true feelings and explore the truth. If true opinions are not expressed, then no progression can be made. It should be about NOT JUDGING.

A political stance should not also be a religious one. Politics is group dynamics, not individual, and individual belief is religious in nature.

A theorem designed for group will not work necessarily with an individual. The considerations are entirely different.

Politics is group first, individual second.

Spirituality/personal religion is individual first, group second.

The plural is not the singular.

Liberalism as a political concept applied to the group as an attitude of tolerance is applaudable but when applied to personal morality it is dangerous. It takes no account of feelings. Feelings develop naturally in relationships.

Be conservative in attitude to own relationships, liberal (non judgemental) towards other peoples.

Since the republican movement in the US is so strongly aligned with (fundamental) Christianity, the opposite, democratic movement is then peopled by more liberal types who will not embrace the hyper religious establishmentarianism of the republicans and so via the liberalism comes all other philosophies. New age, paganism, pseudo Hinduism, Buddhism, eastern religions and the occult. Therefore the risk is that church and state are so closely allied in one political party that all members of the other by political definition may be persuaded or forced into other spiritual paths.

This then proves that politics and religion cannot safely co-exist or rather should never be conjoined in this manner.

The polarization of US society will never be solved until they are successfully seen as separate entities.

One a group authority for the people and one a personal matter of experience, as real religion is.

Religious tradition is often more political than spiritual.

Atheism

When looking at the argument of creationism and evolution remember that the point is where we are going, not where we are from. How is our mind now evolving, our consciousness? Arguing apes and monkeys and Adam and eve is a moot point really and merely a distraction. It does not really affect the NOW. It in no way denigrates nor invalidates the life of Jesus Christ as an example to inspire all mankind. Life of Jesus Christ and son ship with God is a totally different issue. Going round and round in circles talking about dinosaurs is not going to help you love your neighbour. Dawkins must remember his intention. He cannot disprove god by disproving the biblical interpretation of creation. He does not address the difference between the body, mind and spirit nor the capacity for spirituality. He addresses only human religion.

If he does disprove God in the eyes of some believers, what will he replace it with? Christianity empties you then fills you again with something bigger than you thought possible. What will Dawkins fill you with afterward? Without God there is only the ego.

But freedom of ego is no freedom at all. It is a stagnant trap.

Freedom of ego quickly disintegrates into non- adaptation to environment and short term choices of developing levels of obvious power and on a more obvious level, addictive behaviours which quickly cannot be sated and so follows a state of ennui through non spiritual advancement, no challenge, no tests for character. A framework of moral behaviour, a target of perfection, a recognition of TRUTH   (God) is needed to prevent this. There is only real freedom within boundaries.

We are animals but we are not, we reason, we sympathise, we resonate with truth, we worship, we make sentient choices.

Atheism does not deal with the reason why we have spiritual tendencies. It seeks to deny only.

Most science is what has been proved to be tangibly true, nothing more. It cannot measure what has NOT yet been proved to be true or been measured. Indeed, many techniques have yet to be discovered if science is to be what it is purported to be true - that is the truth.

(Theoretical science is concerned with academic perception and extrapolation of already discovered facts.)

Science is used by atheists as a weapon, yet it is only lent to them. Atheists do not own science, Darwinian theories et al do not BELONG to them, and ironic of course that atheism itself is a religion which has defined itself in and as the shadow and rejection of other world monotheistic religions. It is the lack of them and so owes to them its very existence and has kidnapped Darwinian science as its own sacred scripture in a bid to convert.

The atheistic agenda is to force and introduce a viewpoint of the church which is extreme. To draw a dichotomy which allows the atheistic viewpoint to absorb and occupy the reasonable territory in between. That is why they use science as a tool. Science is mostly reasonable, and is seen as such.

Between where science ends and atheism begins is opinion. Science is a technique that can be used by anybody. Atheism does not own science; it does not belong to them.

Man needs to aspire, to look upwards and forwards, atheism maybe just distracting itself with destruction whilst not giving a thought to what would happen if it actually managed to kill belief in a higher being. The worst form of terrorism. Atheism has forgotten it's most serious consideration- if it manages to remove the god concept from the world, what will it be taking away from mankind? And what then will take its place? Within religion is the quest for understanding and our purpose.

Science is concerned with the past, what has been physically proven. In spite of theoretical quantum physics, the more spiritual questions such as where does the seat of consciousness reside have not been answered, because they lie in the spiritual domain.

Nor has life been CREATED, only copied, CLONED using the existing laws of nature, never ORIGINATED by science. Science cannot CREATE these laws, it can only ABIDE by and try and MEASURE them.

———————————————————————

God is beyond human associations. Logic is a construct of the human mind, born of a linear temporal existence and based on reference.

———————————————————————

Why do we learn?

What is the purpose?

Our bodies age and decay but our characters grow and progress through our decisions and actions, if there is no life after death why does this happen?

Animal souls? Do animals have a soul? Criteria?

Do they make moral decisions? / Choices? Or purely from instinct – from hunger – fear.

'Why is there so much suffering in the world if there is a God?'

If we are just purely all just biological material beings we wouldn't care and would be pleased at our consequent advantage from others of our species dying.

Atheism will continue to try and prove truth itself, but as only God can prove truth, as the source and the constant of it, it can never be done, only through faith, and by feeling through experience.

Feeling, emotion, faith, and recognition of truth cannot be quantified solely by cold intellect.

The occult

People attempting to control the environment and other people through psychological and occult techniques cannot possibly know the full effect of what they are trying to cause, especially when playing with the wills of others. It is dangerous. The controller is as much in bondage as the person being controlled. Doubly so in fact as he still must control himself also.

The occult is not dangerous in itself, only in the hands of intent, as the tendency seems to be to always let the ego take over and quickly the occult 'student' typically attempts to change his environment and even people to suit his own desires rather than learning to adapt to them. This is the trap.

'White magic' does not have to exist to oppose black. 'Black magicians' will soon fall to the consequences of their own meddling if left to
run their course.

Magic is about Neuro-linguistic programming/ psychological manipulation, intent and belief on behalf of the recipient/victim and practitioner but ultimate personal power can only come through a proper adjutant relationship and alliance with God as the ultimate power in the universe.

Not all power is about appearing powerful. Obvious power being generally being dark and ego-driven. True power is not immediately obvious. (Evil is shallow).

Objects do not contain power; they can only represent it to feeble and believing minds. From magic fetishes used in psychological trickery, to the newest car, the latest sofa, attempting to confer status through the illusion of material success.

The dark occult is ultimately using all your power to create a web of influence which ultimately must be protected and maintained (through mental and psychological effort) constantly as though it is an extra limb. Control and intent make the externalisation of this kind of power dangerous.

There is no scientific system, spell, process of thinking or manipulation of energies which has not been designed by God as part of his creation. Therefore there is only one shortcut to achieve maximum personal power in the universe and that is to engage with the will of God and live out your life to his plan. He is the source of all.

Hierarchically available knowledge is manipulative and open to abuse, absorption of knowledge is controlled by the level of a person's own wisdom and is healthily selective to that person anyway, so restricted knowledge is always agenda based and can be damaging.

The nature of truth

Truth is rarely convenient.

You can only have faith IN YOUR own body and mind, not the image of anyone else's, also have faith in God. He is truth. Faith in God is faith in truth. That is why all must try and be guided by him. Through experiencing truth, we experience God.

Morality dictates wrong and right, black and white. Right is aligned with truth. Wrong with lies and manipulation. Truth is singular, not plural. It is not dependent upon individual memory or perception but by the guidance of our inner spirit. You cannot abuse truth to support your own perception. That is utterly wrong, though a choice we have. Truth is greater than a dispute and an argument. Truth is what actually happens and what God observes. He tells us, when we try and hear, in our hearts. We can feel and know truth when we experience it. It is the driving purpose of our lives. Truth is divine, perfect. It is of God. It resonates throughout all of us through the (our) universe back to him. It literally rings true inside us. For he is in us.

It is not enough to think truth you have to feel it.

Truth cannot be explained or measured by cold analysis, only by personal experience; it cannot be reduced to a perspective. It is at once individual and common to all, and so is an eternal value, the expressions 'there is no truth', or 'everyone has their own truth', is a fallacy and a manipulation. Truth has its own resonance which as creatures of the universe we can all feel (resonating).

Recognition of the truth destroys (potential) evil.

If you have experienced truth, you have experienced God.

Is it desirable to be a good liar?

Lying suspends reality (reality avoidance). It is a technique to be one's own God. When we lie we create and then must further defend, maintain and shore up an alternate reality against other personalities.

It stops us moving and reacting in harmony with the events of reality (the world we live in). We also take the recipients of our own lies into our own falsely created world and prevent them from reacting properly to or learning from events in the world also. It is a sin against ourselves and them and an attempted triumph of ego over truth. It is an attempted defence against change and adaptation.

The laws of reflectivity mean that lies can be detected. The eyes as always are windows into the soul. The mind is a mirror reflecting the world and us into it. We cannot hide the truth from those who are receptive to it and have determined to live in it.

A lie is a falsified and invented experience, a story which never took place and so no truth may be learned from it as it is a denial of true experience for ourselves and others. It may become a false memory if perpetuated which is problematic.

A lie has not been lived, only imagined by one being and that entirely bound by the limits of his ego and consequent imagination. Truth can only be experienced by living.

There is in fact a singular truth, all humans resonate with this on a spiritual level and move in relativity to it. It is not the other way about - that is - one man and many truths as then there would be no need for moral behaviour and therefore no spiritual advancement. Nor is it a new perspective on a bad moral choice, which allows you to keep doing it with justification even though it is bad for you and possibly others, especially if they love you. Those choices or tendencies instead must be eradicated through new habit and reaction formation and unhelpful ones discarded. Transformation and replacement instead of a new perspective.

When you move in relativity with someone you have a relationship, not an 'experience'. Saying it is an 'experience' allows you morally to become a detached observer and therefore detached from your own moral responsibilities to that relationship. You can have an 'experience' with an object, but between two people (personalities) there is always relationship and therefore feelings and consequent responsibilities.

Thinking moves to feeling moves to acting – conceptually, and in truth.

Think about something, observe it and realise it as truth, feel it as truth and act it out in truth into the world.

If you seek truth you seek God.

Never accept anything as truth until you have experienced it as such, but if you hear and know it, never ignore it, regardless of its source.

The cause is just as much the truth as the effect.

If you live in times of adversity, you will become much more sensitive to truth, it is easy to adapt to good times, but hardships forge strong wills and keener perceptions.

There is much evil in the world, as we all have free will, but divine justice is slow but sure. There are natural consequences to perpetuating iniquity and the truth, in the end, cannot be hidden.

No-one is powerless, everyone has the power to act in truth and emancipate others from illusion and falsehood. If you act in truth, you are representing God.

Because God is the truth, he is also the constant.

As we must be humble before God we must be humble before the truth and also before others as God and therefore the truth is in us all.

Truth is the ultimate power.

Martial arts as relationship

You cannot effectively defeat an opponent with hate. As we all feel truth, righteous anger is a far more effective force as it carries with it a sense of divine judgement and love. If you hate u cannot understand your opponent as love comes from understanding, not hate.

Hate comes from a refusal to understand.

So if u hate you have not understood your opponent and so you fight within
yourself and will never really defeat him, if you beat him he will fear you but not respect you.

A warrior's battle cry after killing an opponent is a denial of what he has just done.

In martial arts, action follows breath.

Always treat multiple opponents as one enemy as they are of one mind to harm you and so defeat the leader, you will then defeat the group.

In fighting, or in any endeavour, there will always be someone better because each person thinks differently. If someone thinks more deeply they will be better. Fighting is thinking, it betrays the way you think, it betrays personality, it reflects your dominant emotion and your approach to life and relationships. When you are fighting there is no hiding, whatever skills you have you will use those that reflect the person you are.

+————————————————————————

When considering that when you fight with monsters you should be careful that as a result you do not become a monster yourself, we should add to that - 'or invent monsters to fight when there are none around'. When afraid of the violent, it is your own awareness of the similar violence in yourself which is scary.

+————————————————————————

A sword is not a weapon on its own.

+————————————————————————

Real power is that that does require conscious over control, a teenager being angry is internally focused. A punch with contractive physical power that feels mighty to the deliverer feels feeble to the recipient yet often a really externalised punch - TOTALLY externalised without the deliverer 'hanging on' to feel his own power through ego, is absolutely powerful as you have delivered all of yourself, outside yourself.

+————————————————————————

There are no such things as attack and defence, only as far as a moral judgement. There is only action and reaction.

A hard spirit is more desirable in combat than hard hands, hard hands can be broken against your will, but your spirit cannot.

The martial art is only as effective as the martial artist who uses it.

When you fight someone, because of speed there is no hiding your true self it is all genuine reaction.

Fighting is visualisation, done in the mind then performed with the body and spirit.

When we fight we are fighting to find out the truth about ourselves. It is a reflective activity, like any encounter between two personalities.

The blow is just the connection, the energy transferred afterwards through the connection made is the damage, movement of chi, and intent controls the energy.

Fighting is spirit focused as it is always a relationship in personality which furthers understanding of yourself on different levels through time.

The purpose of defeat is to learn. Seppuku is further self defeating because it allows the person concerned to escape the learning process and not face and conquer his ego.

Martial arts are not necessarily a brutal pastime. As a physical therapy for exposing emotional problems such as lack of confidence in self or over aggressiveness it can be invaluable as when sparring you cannot hide true response and these physical responses manifest automatically.
As these responses filter upward from the physical to the emotional, as they were learnt as a child, so they can be healed using the same process.
You must change the INTENT of the sparring to do this.

This works as fighting is a reflective activity as any encounter between two personalities is.

It is hard enough winning an argument when you know you are in the wrong, let alone a fight. Unless you fight blindly.

True Christianity empowers & concentrates your power thru discipline. Your character becomes powerful & focused, not weak & disparate. In life you become like the advanced martial artist breaking rocks with his hands.

Through adaptation and focus, you conquer life.

The rest

We have a spirit, but we also have a mind, the science of the way our psychology works is very exacting. Spirituality does not convey a complete negation of negative psychological issues necessarily. Often we are healed through contact with others. God will often require us to take steps to cure ourselves of our own issues before he deigns to do it for us. Again, that way we learn and further see that we are capable of conquering ourselves.

Your mind is a filter between your spirit and the world which works both ways. The mind is material, the spirit is not. Though both are created by God.

Breathing, relaxation and techniques of maintaining the body's fitness are not necessarily 'evil' and it is ridiculous to presume so.

The world wants you to live from consuming one thing to the next, to depend on these things for the happiness of yourself and your family.

Always take regular time to be thankful and appreciative for what you already have rather than focusing constantly on gaining something else.

Being 'born again' could be understood as the point at which spiritual values become more important to you than material ones.

For a philosophy to work in practice there must be room for expansion.

You cannot enforce respect through fear.

Hypnotism glosses over the effect but does not eradicate the cause.

A placebo is the focus for a mind to heal through.

Men make contradictions, God does not.

Everyone has something unique to give this world.

Respect leads to love, fear leads to hate.

Someone who has trouble imagining a higher being has a head too small to contain him and an ego too big to admit him. You must have the ability to place understanding outside yourself. If you cannot place understanding outside yourself you cannot fully understand others.

Beware of anyone who keeps a pretence of being perfect, they are the most dangerous of all - they are lying to themselves as well as you. If you want to teach be humble before your own shortcomings. Such spiritual teachers should want you to be as happy as YOU can be, not as happy as THEY are.

It is never too late to take the right step. Though it may be a different one due to circumstances, it will still be in the same correct direction.

We must all go on from where we are. We ordinarily cannot turn back the clock and go on. We can live neither in the past or the future. However, real forgiveness, whether of others or oneself, provides a fresh start, and along with hindsight, also an informed one.

Instead of just moving forward and not looking back, true forgiveness allows us to move sideways.

Forgiving other people is hard to apply sometimes as it means admitting your own guilt in the situation which sometimes people play out through deep seated control dramas they don't want to recognise.

Emotions are fleeting, the body constant, and the spirit eternal.

Philosophy should be an earnest and sincere search for the truth for all, not an exercise in intellectual acrobatics and/or masturbation of ego. It is not a competition of cleverness.

Spiritual values cannot be quantified by a material system of logic. Science cannot evaluate the nature of God as it cannot even evaluate human consciousness, much less a higher being than ourselves. It is simply a system for understanding the world from a material viewpoint.

As a loving father does, God grants us the means (strength, courage, wisdom etc) to solve our own problems rather than fix them for us.

Look to the durable and experienced to find wisdom. Those who have been through the most delve the deepest into life.

Acts of service to others soon distract from one's own issues. Allowing you then to see them more objectively and so how to solve them more clearly.

God grants us talents and activities we love to inform us of the direction he wishes us to lead our lives in.

True power does not make you feel POWERFUL, it makes you feel FREE.

Wisdom is knowing when to stand strong and when to bend and flow with the pressure.

It should be reflected in the choices you make for yourself as well as in your advice for others.

From the most heinous of experiences can come the most experiential wisdom, if we learn.

Things are really NOT always what they seem. Be satisfied with your own life. Be creative within the boundaries of yourself and so get to know yourself. Do not try and live someone else's life or attempt to be someone other than who you are. Neither be arrogant enough to presume to know someone else's level of real happiness and therefore become envious of something they do not actually possess.

The severity of problems is measured purely in the manner in which you deal with them.

Obsession comes through trying to control what is outside of your own power to control.

If the devil has a plan it is to addict and befuddle men through short term pleasures and unearned power. To draw men away from spiritual goals and towards the desires of the ego.

To make man believe the only way out of the material world's problems is to go further into them. Our depressions, our sadness.

But these have a spiritual basis so they can only be cured by attaining spiritual values and breaking the cycle of materialism. That is God's plan.

Islam's great strength is a strict structure and male empowerment.

To live is to make mistakes, to learn.

A display of positive power (e.g.) a monk influencing and shaping snowflakes and crystals is not akin to real kindness. It does not feed or house or effectively counsel a person in real need. It is only ambient, energetic and aesthetic in nature.

Real spiritual power is socialised, service orientated, expressed in terms of others, not just personalised and mystical.

We are gregarious beings as:

We all reflect one another and so we need others to define ourselves.

We all contain the divine spark.

Our spiritual path is effectively null if not socialised.

Due to reflectivity, we need others as a reference point to contextualise ourselves, to expose and repair our neuroses.

Be aware of what you'd rather believe to suit your own ego.

To be an effective artist, push your intention through your instrument/medium, then let OTHERS judge your work.

The difference between grey areas and absolutes is the passage of time.

Instead of demonstrating a piece of technology or purely some skill with an object you possess, demonstrate always a virtue you possess – e.g. patience, kindness - that is of the kingdom of God, the other world, a spiritual possession you can carry with you and use everywhere without dependence on anything or anyone else.

People may possess particular skills in other areas but it is no guide to their level of sincerity or goodness.

NLP as a tool for self escape against issues only has limited uses; all problems must be dealt with in their entirety sooner or later.

Militant religions attract adherents through tradition, structure and empowerment.

Mantras and chants are just a way to focus a certain level of mind so that other thoughts and realisations maybe seen, experienced. It is like closing your eyes and all other senses become sharper. It is a positive distraction technique.

If you have a centre, everything arranges itself naturally around that. Maintaining a proper moral and spiritual centre in life is therefore fundamental to success.

In relationships, wandering from one to another is consistently unbalancing. You should become balanced in yourself between them to make sure you can cope with the extra weight of one. You must be RELATIVELY balanced in yourself with the truth before you can balance with another.

Being at your best under pressure is about no time to think, you react revealing the proper strength of your personality with none of the insecurities that may normally occur.

Initial Entrance into the kingdom of God is based on intention, not achievement, intention to find God.

It is never weak to follow God, or in other words to attempt perfection. God is the measure of perfection. Christ is an inspiration to achieve that perfection in your life. When you have more adversity in your life than most, you cannot help but look for higher and deeper truths to answer your questions.

Good flows from bad, if you allow it.

When you feel powerless all the better as then concerns and problems are in God's hands and he is infinitely better equipped to deal with them than you are. Literally.

Each of us must serve something greater. Man reaches for higher values and meanings to improve his life experience and creates God if he is not already there. This 'God' maybe money, power, fame, atheism (worship of the self and ego and opposition to a higher force, celebrity etc).

We all grow toward spirit not back into more material states; the material world is temporal and bound by physics - space and time. The body is a vehicle to be taken care of, but not the ultimate goal; it is the means to an end, not the end in itself.

Emotional intelligence:	Academic intelligence:
Reactive- very quick/ unconscious	Cognitive- slow and analytical
Subtractive- purely takes from immediate situation	Additive- danger of adding to situation due to ego bias
Adaptive	Rigid/ structured
	Abstractive- alternatives
	Objective- able to take a step back

Is one of these slower than the other? If so, which comes first? Does the person with more E.I. have a more impulsive character? Does one follow behind the other? Are they different aspects of the same thing?

The mind is the energetic but still material-bound product of the electro- chemical activities of the body and is the mechanism whereby the human spirit interfaces with the world. The mind produces choices and the spirit chooses. The spirit being 'you'.

Technology we create mirrors the functions of the human mind which is like a computer, which can take photographs, record films, record audio and play it back at will in our memory.

We don't all have to go through the same levels to reach the same place.

Infinite vagerities of personality endowment, capacity for will decision, moral choice and intent all affect the progress of each mortal through the levels of spiritual attainment.

The glory of God - the most direct manifestation of which is the existence of love within the human race. We are all indwelt by God; this is his blessing, his divine and perfect guide within us.

Do not judge someone based solely on their belief system. Remember they are an imperfect work in progress personality just as you are, as well as a representative of a faith structure.

Faith is actualised hope.

The hardest thing to find in this world is consistency/constancy.

The evil of magic is that instead of compromising yourself and being willing to change, it is an attempt to compromise the world to your own will so you may remain static/unchanged.

The reasons why you think that people like you may not be the same as the reasons why they do.

An imagination encompasses the possibilities of the universe it was born into.

There is no such thing as a consistently good liar; liars must mix the truth with lies to be effective.

Black and white both contain all colours.

The only point of human experience is to extrapolate spiritual meaning and significance from it.

Learning is spiritual. Time is the tool for learning.

Whether the experience is good or bad the spiritual benefit may not tally likewise. In fact the 'blessing' derived is usually counter to whether the experience is a happy and immediately enjoyable one.

If you depend on other's behaviours for your happiness, you will always be seeking to control and will never learn to control yourself.

Realise you are human, and if you did not make mistakes you would never learn. Making mistakes is a learning system. Try not to make the same mistake twice.

'Experience' has become an insidious excuse for justifying bad behaviour, undermining morality.

God judges by observing INTENT, man judges by observing CHOICE.

Just because it's a popular opinion does not mean it's incorrect.

Civilisation has become an end in itself instead of the means to achieve it.

Imperfections, not perfections are what bind us in love.

The inverse reaction to our own natural reaction is often what is required.

People are only ever inspired by another's intention. Force of personality is constrictive, not expansive - (cult of personality, power, and control).

Be interested in what you feel, not what other people think.

A teacher does not teach their own mistakes but fosters your own perfected technique.

The world is not uniform and rigid but irregular and responsive, so there are no perfect learning or operating systems. Only good tools to manufacture a personal system. You must again, adapt.

The adoption of projecting a false image of social fragrantness and constant capable nirvana is rooted in the rape of self image and consequent constant absolute control. People bend themselves for social acceptance at the expense of an inner path. It's an attempt to individualise, isolate and standardise. Arrogance and lack of humility rule in this kind of created, marketed world. People consume more in order to maintain themselves in the eyes of their peers as some advertised status quo. They only live externally in regards to their self image and internally through lack of real emotional contact with others.

Intention is the most important and powerful concept in this world, it is the manner in which we are divinely judged, it is through intention that we can influence and form and create the world and ourselves. Intention is powerful. Intention with intent is more powerful still.

Aloneness is altogether different from loneliness; we may feel lonely, but not alone, if only in that loneliness.

Defeat is just as good tool as victory. (Better in fact, for learning).

Emphasis on the individual at the expense of the community is evil. (Emphasis of the community at the expense of the individual is also evil.)

You cannot live and truly understand through detached observation and avoidance of experience, your only reference point you then have is your own ego (Buddhism etc).

Learn to take your own advice, practice what you preach.

To be an effective person one must be able to operate as a whole, and part of a whole.

Great art is produced on behalf of mankind not on behalf of the author.

Happiness is being happy with the path you are on.

You cannot truly know yourself except through others, we reflect each other.

Racism involves an assumption of both bad ancestry and a belief in a type of reincarnation, in that a person can be made a focal point or distillate of all negative actions of his forefathers, and made scapegoat to such, though he may be innocent himself. It is a sweeping and low form of judgement that diminishes the divine spark within the victim and not only denigrates him as less than human, but less than God has granted him, and therefore it is a crime against God.

Understanding is the foundation and first tenet of love.

As arrogance increases, wisdom diminishes.

Wisdom cannot help you unless you act in accordance with it.

Nothing of the self dies, change does not kill parts of the self, it only balances them differently.

The reason why Christ did not have children is because any man can have children, but Jesus was son of God incarnate, not man incarnate, so at once his genes would not carry his 'Godhood' necessarily, which leaves the question why did he not have children? Because he would not be able, as a son of God and perfect father, to be a perfect physical and spiritual father to any mortal children in an imperfect environment, and also the fact his CHILDREN would be viewed as divine even if they were not, and a Man-God having children would necessitate teaching teachings beyond the worlds readiness at the time.

Also if Jesus knew he was to die early, why would he have kids? Seems slightly irresponsible.

The answer always lies in the opposite. Within your weakness lies your strength, within your strength lies your weakness.

Can the answers be found in popular opinion or an academic specific, which is to say; is your belief in this the truth or just your tendency?

Holding an alternative view is often more about the ego than the actual beliefs of that person. Flying in the face of a strong convention will draw a marked comparison that people often capitalise upon whether it is good for them or not.

Just as it is not good to be totally *un*accepting of all concepts and situations, neither is it good and can be just as damaging to be totally accepting.

Would you rather trust someone who has made mistakes and learnt the correct path from the consequences or someone who has yet to fall?

Lies and deceit create frission and spark new but illusory relationships, this behaviour is infectious, and could not honesty and patience be spread instead?

Post modernists often just others with absolutism whilst judging themselves with a 'shades of grey' or 'own truth' policy.

God knows the end and shows us the beginning.

Will life become more and more convenient or will old values come full circle and reassert themselves?

Always seek out the meek, they have nothing to lose but each other and so have little to lose whereas the more people possess the less compassion they have and the more fear of losing their own status.

Honest people provide the basis for irreverent and ironic/sarcastic comedy; they are the root of life.

The difference between a scientist and a priest is: The scientist cannot see further than his own nose and the priest does not realise he has one.

Fashion *can* be understood as an attempt to pre-empt others judgement of oneself.

The concept of karma is a method of judging.

Christians share a God and Buddhists share a thought. Is the west so enamoured with God because Jesus was in the Middle East? And vice versa?

Accept a level of knowledge; no-one knows the whole truth. Saying you know what is happening in the war in Iraq is like saying you know what is happening in a house down the street.

Journalism is spin. Just as law, journalists are lawyers.

Everyone is learning the same lessons all the time.

Buddhist inspiration is impersonal, Christian inspiration is personal. i.e. Can there be a Buddhist martyr?

Particles are not tendencies they are intentions, or perhaps tendencies which must be moved and established, given purpose in reality by intention.

Quantum physics is part science and part religion.

Observer in science, participant in religion.

Evil is based on the obvious; it is by no means deep.

Knowledge cannot be taken from you, once you have it, it is part of you, you will always possess it, especially if you have felt it through experience, then it becomes truth and therefore wisdom.

We are always at our best when living under oppression (Boundaries within which to grow).

Let god be responsible for your own power, then you are never scared of losing it. God grants it when needed.

There are no shades of grey; there are just options before choices. Choices are absolute, do or do not. Once you have made a choice, you have made it, it has become an absolute, and it is part of history.

True and False Liberty, 'Black and white' - 'shades of grey'

The physical world has rules, as has the psychology of humans.

The human mind needs reference points to function, like triangulation on a map in forming opinions and boundaries.

Other people make up very important reference points. Imagine what it would be like in the world if there were only you. We need human contact to define ourselves and give ourselves context.

Conceptual living on an anarchic 'makeup your own rules, amoral, there is no black and white and only shades of grey' basis leads to psychological abuse and manipulation, rather there are no shades of grey , only shade of black and white. Ultimately there is always a choice in actuality of whether to do A or B. So choice requires black or white. Do this or do that. Do or do not.

Creativity within a system with no boundaries is less creative as there are no reference points. It is also a fallacy as the artist by virtue of his own experience already has boundaries; he is also bound by those of his own personality and his medium. As soon as a piece becomes complete it is crystallised as a style and then by influence ultimately a movement, by which it is categorised, therefore escape from categories and association is impossible as this is the way the reality works by our perceptions.

You are only truly powerful when you cannot feel your own power- When it is extended out into the world. When you are 'in' it and can feel it, no-one else can unless you find perfect balance and the power resonates between you and the world.

People wanting to feel powerful often divest themselves of real power because of their ego which blinds them to the effect (often self destroying) they are having upon the world and people around them. The great battle of every human is the spirit versus the ego.

You can only truly gain power by relinquishing it.

The world is a mirror which reflects you.

You must have a sense of self before you can project yourself.

If you want good advice, ask someone who has faced the situation already.

Experience is the best teacher.

A large ego is good when it serves you well but it can be disastrous when it does not. Ego does not seek to adapt. Arrogance seeks to control and bend to its will.

Money cannot love you back.

In human relationships, you should be with someone who brings out the best in you and vice versa. Someone who has a shared agenda.

However, this does not necessarily mean someone who you have just good times with.

The best in yourself is spiritual values

To manifest these you must first and foremost share truth with each other which sometimes requires conflict. Sharing truth and honesty and respect produces true understanding which leads to real lasting love.

It is not about your ego having a free ride.

Faith relationships often last longer because of a shared agenda, shared morality, shared purpose, shared belief.

Love and obedience are two different things. Love is not slavish.

There does not have to be a heaven or hell when we leave this world as the law of duality does not have to exist outside our temporal reality. Re: this is why hell doesn't have to exist. As the devil is not the equal of God, so in the spiritual world there is not necessarily an equal and opposite reaction to a force as in the material one. Earthly physics do not apply to spirit.

Is human sexuality mutable? And can change? Or is it absolute and fixed?

The only worthy personal investment is in skills and values.

Time is only relevant to experience when it comes to the human mind.

Sexually addictive behaviour is bad because it is materially and sexually obsessive and therefore it retards spiritual progress, keeping choices bound to the animal instincts and the material plane.

During 'casual' sex, perversions replace love. What a person mechanically likes is how it begins, then emotional avoidance techniques like domination and submissiveness.

Would you rather be with someone who was constant and reliable, or someone who was fickle and prey to their own emotions? The person who has a belief system has a conscious framework rather than just one based on mood.

Christianity is a deconstructive and then reconstructive religion. A material decision which negates the spiritual can take the spirit way off course.

'Whatever will be will be' (fatalism) tends to disregard free will.

Betrayal begins in the mind; sex with a third party is always good when you are already connected with someone else but very wrong. It robs the proper partner of their very energy and life force.

What a third party is after in that situation is the love which has been given to you by someone else, not you as yourself.

People have their own agendas; God is only ever after what is best for you.

You cannot go in without recognition of the without. (God is both an external and independent and an internal personal force).

Pantheism gives short term liberal freedom and power which eventually traps the spirit where as Christian belief gives long term spiritual power with perhaps little direct material gain in our temporal world.

Addiction to chaos is a distraction and a habit which prevents stillness and facing the self.

Anxiety is a by-product of fear and tranquillity is a by-product of love.

Eastern religions – Buddhism/Hinduism etc – offer a new perspective on what one is doing in one's life.

Many people prefer a belief system which offers position and status. Many times in a bid to attract followers a belief system will state that an individual has special powers. Power which does not need to be earned is a very seductive draw to someone who is searching. There is then no need to be humble.

For instance, mediums in the spiritualist church. Faith healers.

(Some also in the Christian church).

Many females become Wiccans to worship the female.

We don't all have to go through the same levels to get to the same place. We are all different and some inherent qualities allow us past certain problems easily.

Letting go is not letting go of objects and possessions it is letting go of fears and control –

Needless material possessions are just a manifestation of the wrong attitude.

People who don't believe in God may blame him when something goes wrong nonetheless.

Just as people who don't believe turn to him for help in times of trouble.

Don't constantly magnify the negative for others by drawing attention to it.

No sacred scripture is infallible. You cannot fit God in a book. Only an approach to him. God must be experienced.

Self - conviction is the only kind that works to change you. Conviction by others does not.

In the absence of god self worship can occur.

Patience, love, endurance, you cannot touch them but they are a reality. A reality of the spirit. People possess values & attributes just as they have possessions you can touch.
You just have to realise that you recognise them with your spirit rather than your hands.

Forgiveness allows us to move on and keep adapting, keep changing. Being unforgiving makes us unable to move on and keeps us static.

God can save you, no matter how low you feel you have fallen. But you must intend to save yourself and you must TRY.

When you are 'born again' you start again as a child. You must learn to live by God's plan for you, not your own, however there is no better personality to be responsible for the consequences of the decisions in your life than an all- knowing, all seeing higher being you can communicate with on a personal level.

The physical nature of a person is of only short term importance in a relationship.

There is a definite you, which is your spirit. Your mind is a possession. An interface with the world.

You can never see the full effect of your own deeds.

This is the end of my book's journey, thank you for reading and I hope you received something from doing so, whether it was challenge, revelation or just entertainment.

Above all this book was written to promote TRUTH in the reader.

May you all be blessed, whomever and wherever you are.

Charlie Fox

Autumn '09

Nottingham

England

These blank pages are for your own notes:

Lightning Source UK Ltd.
Milton Keynes UK
UKHW040736140919
349756UK00002B/3/P